The Homeless Motivational Speaker

by George Carroll

DEDICATION

To my family: Mom, Dad, Ray III and Jessie. Your unconditional support for me and my work means the world to me. I love you all.

To my fans: Thank you for sticking with me and supporting me through all the ups and downs. I love you all.

To YOU: The reader, who has a dream and an unconquerable spirit. Never let any limitation or obstacle stand in the way of you having your dreams. I sincerely hope this book can be just a small example of what's possible when you never give up. And remember, your own personal transformation contributes to the world.

"Personal transformation can and does have global effects. As we go, so goes the world, for the world is us. The revolution that will save the world is ultimately a personal one."
— Marianne Williamson

CONTENTS

INTRODUCTION

I had tunnel vision. I couldn't see the forest through the trees...There I was, living in a 300 square-foot studio apartment infested with bed bugs. The smell of failure reeked in my apartment, and I was crying my eyes out. Snot was running out of my nose and I could feel the gut-wrenching pain of self-judgment, disgust and blame.

I was broke; about to go bankrupt and near homelessness...What was I going to do? Most of my belongings weren't salvageable, and I knew I was going to lose pretty much everything I owned. I was devastated...

"Two roads diverged in a wood and I - I took the one less traveled by; and that has made all the difference."
- Robert Frost

This book is an adventure - a roller-coaster ride that will inspire you, frustrate you and hopefully open new doors of possibility. The river of life takes us on a phenomenal ride and sometimes, the only true freedom is to surrender to it.

What if your life wants to look like no other life being lived on the planet? Are you willing to create your life without using other people's lives as a way to compare and contrast your life? Are you willing to surrender to your greatness?

You are a unique composition of magic, unlike anything that has ever existed in the history of the Universe. The combination of experiences, wisdom, knowledge and awareness you have doesn't exist anywhere else in the cosmos. Remember this - no one knows what you know like you know it.

Consider that every choice that you've ever chosen, you chose with pure psychic brilliance; because you knew on some level, those choices, no matter what they created, either fed a capacity, gave you more awareness or contributed to a greater future.

Consider that each of those choices brought you to this precise moment. And consider that this precise moment is the perfect launching point for you to create the rest of your life from. Every moment has the potential to be the beginning of something great.

I hope this book ignites something within you that helps you on your adventure of life. I wish you infinite levels of joy and happiness. And most of all, I hope my story helps you find more freedom to choose your own path, no matter what it looks like.

Lovin' you like the badass you are…
Mad Love,
George Carroll

"Here's To The Crazy Ones. The misfits. The rebels. The trouble-makers. The round pegs in the square holes. The ones who see things differently.

They're not fond of rules, and they have no respect for the status-quo. You can quote them, disagree with them, glorify, or vilify them.

About the only thing you can't do is ignore them. Because they change things. They push the human race forward. And while some may see them as the crazy ones, we see genius.

Because the people who are crazy enough to think they can change the world - are the ones who do."

— Steve Jobs (1955 - 2011)

1
A DREAM IS BORN

"All our dreams can come true, if we have the courage to pursue them."
— Walt Disney

Empty Your Cup

A buddhist monk was sitting with a young protege. After a short conversation, the monk noticed something.

To teach him a lesson, he began to pour hot tea into his tea cup. The tea began to spill over and onto the table, then onto the protege's lap.

The protege yelped, *"stop pouring, my cup is full, my cup is full!"*

The monk said, *"That's exactly how your mind is. Full of your own assumptions and full of your own conclusions about life. If you want to become great, you must empty the cup of your mind."*

There I was, living in a 300 square-foot studio apartment infested with bed bugs. I was crying my eyes out and I was broke as a joke. I was near bankruptcy and homelessness.

More on that later...

When I was 4 years old, a dream was born.

You see, I'm just a kid from the small town of Pueblo, Colorado and at a very young age, I knew what I wanted to do when I grew up.

My Dream was to play Professional Football.

Have you ever felt something, or touched something and your very being was moved by it? Was it unreasonable for me to think I could play professional football?

In 1984, I tried on my first helmet and held my first football and something magical happened. It was like my future was downloaded into my little brain and the next 18 years of my life were written, but the 18th year would end in heart-breaking fashion.

My hero growing up was Jerry Rice - the best wide-receiver to ever play the game of pro-football. I grew up in a neighborhood where most of the kids were older than me, so I had to step my game up to play at their level.

Because of this, by the time I was playing organized little league football at 8 years old, I was years ahead of my age group and I stood out from the crowd.

The first time I touched a football in little league, I ran a kick-off return for a touchdown. It just seemed so easy. Each year, I was always the MVP of my team. I just somehow knew how to play the game faster than everyone else.

I just "saw" the game differently. I sometimes knew what was going to happen even before it happened. By the time I was in middle school, it seemed the whole city of Pueblo knew who I was.

Also, in middle school, I was hanging out with a group of kids who were the "trouble-makers" of the school. And because I wanted to fit in a be liked by them, I finally broke into peer-pressure and started drinking and doing drugs by the age of 13.

"Who you hang out with is who you become."
— Tony Robbins

My grades started to drop and my dedication to my dream was also starting to diminish. It was my first lesson in seeing how much our peer groups influence our choices and behaviors.

The outlook wasn't good for me. I was arrested for shoplifting and fighting. The people around me who believed in me just looked at me with disappointment.

Thank God for my brother, Ray - He challenged me to play harder and work harder. He also helped keep me out of trouble.

One night when I was 13, my brother showed up at a party I was attending and scolded me for drinking alcohol. I'll never forget that moment. I knew he cared for me and wanted the best for me.

I made it out of middle school safely and I started to surround myself with kids who were more dedicated to sports.

I was also fortunate enough to have a High School football coach who was a phenomenal mentor and leader for me. His name was Keith Lane. His brother Rich Lane also had a huge positive influence in my life.

My dad was always video-taping my games, rooting me on. He attended almost every game I had. He was my biggest fan and my mom was always right by his side.

Without them challenging me, encouraging me and seeing my talents and gifts, I would have never achieved the success I accomplished.

One of the greatest gifts my parents gave me was total freedom. They allowed me to experiment with life and that made a huge difference. I didn't have a curfew and they just let me run wild.

By my sophomore year, I was the starting Wide Receiver for the varsity team and by the end of that year I earned 1st Team All-Conference honors.

By the end of my Junior year, I had broken many of the records in the state of Colorado and I helped take our team to the 2nd round of the playoffs for the first time in school history!

My dream was coming to fruition! I was receiving letters from the major Universities all over the United States:
- University of Colorado
- Colorado State University
- University of Oregon
- University of Texas
- UCLA
- Oklahoma State University
- Kansas State University
- University of Kansas
- University of California
- University of Southern California

And so many more. I couldn't believe it!! My dream was actually coming true!

By my Senior year, I had racked up huge numbers, but unfortunately, our team fell short of the playoffs. I was named All-Colorado as one of the best wide-receivers in the state of Colorado.

As I continued my search for colleges, I remember the feeling in my gut when all the "BIG" Universities turned me away because of my size.

At 5' 7" and 170 pounds, I wasn't your prototypical wide-receiver. Big Universities were looking for 6' 3" 215 pounders and I simply didn't have any more growth in me.

So, I was passed up on all the Division I Universities and I were left with 2 choices:
- North Dakota State University
- University of Northern Colorado

I was devastated. I had my heart set on a Division I school, but my high school coach said something that always stuck with me - because it relates to life too.

"No matter where you are, if you're willing to work hard enough, you can make anything happen."

This statement echoed in my head, and I accepted a scholarship to the University of Northern Colorado, who had just come off of 2 National Championships.

Leaving Pueblo was one of the hardest things I've ever done. As I packed my pickup truck with all of my belongings and with tears in my eyes, I said bye to my family and started driving north.

I remember the song by Green Day, *"time of your life"* was playing on the radio and I broke down into tears on the way to Greeley.

I had to leave everything and everyone I knew and step into a whole new world of uncertainty, and I wasn't sure I could make it as a collegiate athlete. People said, *"you're too small"* and *"you're not fast enough"* …

Were they right?

2
SMALL FISH IN A BIG POND

"Ever since I was a child, I have had this instinctive urge for expansion and growth. To me, the function and duty of a quality human being is the sincere and honest development of one's potential."
— Bruce Lee

Small Fish in a Big Pond

Are you familiar with *The Goldfish Theory?* This theory states that a goldfish can only grow in proportion to the size of its environment...

With tears streaming down my face, I drove myself to Greeley, Colorado where I'd be spending the next 5 years of my life in the pursuit of my dream.

When I arrived and settled in, I went to the gym area early and I was met by a gigantic 250 pound, 6' 6" Aaron Smith who played for the Pittsburg Steelers. I looked up at this massive man and I about sh*t my pants. I realized in that moment I was in for the challenge of a lifetime.

On my first day of practice, I realized that I was the smallest person on the field and I was very intimidated. I felt like Rudy Ruettiger from that movie Rudy.

So, I did the only thing I knew how to do at the time: Work my ass off! I red-shirted my freshman year (which means I learned the system and was a practice only player) and in my first actual year of playing, I backed up the starter, Omar Zuniga, who was a great mentor for me.

We had a great year as a team, and in the off season, I worked my booty off because I knew I was going to be the starter the very next year!

My dream was inching closer and closer!! Could I really play professional football? My 2nd year of playing time came and went and I had one of the best seasons in school history.

I was named 1st Team All-Conference and I was one of the talks of the town. I could taste my dreams!! I was being interviewed by papers and radio shows and everything I had dreamt when I was a kid seemed to be right around the corner.

In the off-season, I worked my butt off and came into the season in the best shape of my life. Faster, stronger and more lean and mean than ever.

The first game of the season, I ran back a kick-off for a touchdown. It reminded me of my first play in little league football many years back.

I had a breakthrough game, but during the 3rd quarter, I suffered 2 sprained ankles that put me out for 2 games.

When I came back, I was a step slower, but I fought my way back. Towards the middle of the season, we had a nationally televised game and I knew it was time for me to shine.

The game was against our rival, AND the other school I was debating attending - The University of North Dakota. I had a record game and scored the winning touchdown!! Because it was nationally televised, I had many eyes on me.

By the end of the season, I was honored 1st Team All-Conference again and the future looked bright!!

Again, I worked hard in the off-season and in the first 3 games of my final year, I shined, and our team was on fire. We were ranked in the Top 25 in the country and on our way to another National Championship.

The middle of the year, I began to question myself, and it showed in my play. I had 3 games in a row where I produced very little, and even though we were winning, my inner demons began eating at me.

Ever since I was little, many people told me that I was too small and not fast enough to be in the NFL. I hated hearing that so I ignored them and kept fighting, but little did I know, those small statements turned into deep, unconscious seeds that would grow over time.

Here's what I realized, looking back: When we get closer and closer to a dream, target, goal or vision, the limitations we've set up for ourselves grow bigger and bigger.

The voices in our heads, the feelings of fear that surface and the fear based images we conjure up - all created from limiting beliefs and judgments that were never ours to begin with. Limitations are learned, we are not born with them.

What happens next changes my life forever, and the choices I make lead me to a lifestyle that make me lucky to be alive today...

3
"SORRY, IT'S OVER"

*"Sometimes, we don't get our dreams,
so we can live our destiny"*
— Tony Robbins

The Dark Forrest

In a magical and powerful kingdom, new kings were elected once in every five years.

After each 5 year tenure, each King is sent into the dark forrest to test his courage and perseverance. So far, no King had survived that forest. After a while, no one wanted to become the King because of the eminent death that awaited.

Finally, one man volunteered to become the King. He reigned for five years, changing the Kingdom for the better. The day came to send him off into the dark forrest. He happily retired his crown to the next King and off he went. Everyone was confused as to why this King was so happy to go into the dark forest. One asked him, *"why are you so happy to die in the dark forrest?"*

The King replied, *"Die? I knew clearly about our custom. So, in the first year, I sent 100 soldiers to kill all the dangerous animals in the forest. In the second year, I sent 500 wood cutters to cut all the trees. In the third year, I sent 1000 farmers to turn the forest into a cultivating land. In the fourth year I sent 2000 villagers to build houses there and settle there. In the fifth year, I built a palace there. Now, there is a new kingdom awaiting me…"*

It was a cloudy day. Windy and there was something eerie about this day.

I was 95-yards short of our school records for yards in a career and on my way to stepping into the vision that I created when was just 4-years old.

I started the game on fire! I felt like I got past those old demons and I had a new zest in my blood. I felt unstoppable and more determined than ever to live my dreams out.

Then…on a harmless run play that was coming from behind me…the unthinkable happened.

As I was blocking the defender in front of me, I planted my right foot firmly into the ground and just as the runner coming from behind me was being tackled by the back end defender, both of their forward momentum toppled my leg and 400 pounds of force and weight came crashing down on my lower leg.

My leg and ankle… shattered.

Everything seemed to happen so fast, until the moment I tried to get up…everything slowed down. I attempted to stand on my feet; I reached down and felt where my leg was completely shattered. I felt the bones shifting in my leg and buckled to the ground, in shock.

A trainer a couple of my teammates carried me off the field and over to the sidelines as the team doctor took off my shoe and sock. What I saw almost made me puke. I looked down to see that my leg and ankle were deformed and then the team doctor looked up at me and said:

"Sorry…it's over."

I burst into tears, along with my teammates who were standing by my side, consoling me. I felt cold and empty. Flashes of childhood memories passed through my mind. All the work, effort, blood, sweat and tears I had put myself through seemed all for nothing.

As they wrapped my leg into a brace to stabilize the break as much as they could, I heard my mom's yelping cries as she ran over to try to console me. I heard my mom, crying her eyes out saying:

"My poor baby…my poor baby!!"

I didn't feel any physical pain, but the emotional pain of knowing that my childhood dream had just come to an end was a blow I wasn't ready to take.

Then, for a moment, something magical happened. As the cart drove off the field and toward the training room, I looked up and saw 7,000 loyal fans sending me off in a standing ovation…cheering and roaring my name!

I began to weep even more. The mixture of feelings I was experiencing was indescribable, and as they drove me off the field for the last time, my High School coaches Keith and Rich were also there in support of me.

The only words that kept repeating in my mind were the words from the team doctor saying, *"Sorry, it's over."*

My advice to you is this - whether you're playing sports in college or the game of life, give it everything you've got.

Don't hold back. Push yourself to the limits and then go a little further. Demand more from yourself every day, because you never know when your last play is going to be. You never know when your last day is going to be.

I had no idea what I wanted to do with my life after that, but I knew it was all going to change. How? Only time would tell…

4
NOW WHAT?

"Nobody can go back and start a new beginning, but anyone can start today and make a new ending."
—Maria Robinson

Healing

When a bone breaks, then heals, it becomes the strongest part of the bone.

When your skin is cut, it forms a scab, then a scar. It becomes the most durable part of that area.

The same can be said with our heart and our emotions. The more we breakdown emotionally, the stronger we become.

I had no idea what I wanted to do with my life. I fell into a state of depression that brought me back into doing drugs and drinking alcohol heavily.

I did my best to drown the pain of feeling like a failure. For the rest of my senior year, I lugged around in crutches, watching my team from the sidelines…helpless.

I pretended I was okay, but I was dying inside. I did my best to rehab my leg, but I never had the same drive inside, and my leg never had the same explosive power it once had.

Yep, it was over. Reality set in deeper and so did the depression.

I graduated with a degree in Communications from The University of Northern Colorado and had no idea as to what I wanted to do. I moved to Denver, CO and started looking for jobs.

5 weeks after I graduated, I found myself without any money and in desperate need of a job. I remember going on a couple of interviews, and I was turned away because I didn't own a suit. So, I went to Arc thrift store to buy a cheap suit for $30 and I started going on more interviews. After a lot of hustling, I was finally hired by a tele-communications company selling high end internet and phone service to small and mid-sized businesses.

I used my depression as fuel to succeed. I had a new motivation and I was ready to tackle the business world. I started off with a bang! I was promoted after my first 6-months into an Assistant Manager.

3 months after that, I was managing a team of 10 sales people, teaching, training and mentoring them to be successful sales people.

I began to fall in love with leading people - teaching, training and leading people to success. I felt invigorated and had a new passion - **teaching and training.**

With my new found passion, I helped take my team from last in the branch to consistently in the top 3. We were on fire and everyone in our branch wanted what we had:
- *Chemistry*
- *Fun*
- *Work Ethic*
- *Genuine Connection with each other*

We were the talk of the town and I was on top of the world! I was making almost $100,000 at 24 years old and doing something that I was passionate about! But there was one problem. I hated my boss and the company but I was in love with my team. Kind of a conflict. My boss came from the military and I did not resonate with his style of leadership. To put it lightly, we butted heads.

But my team loved me because they knew I cared about them. They weren't just a number to me, and my boss had a problem with the way I led, even though I was always producing great results.

After 2 years of mental and emotional corporate abuse, I simply couldn't take it anymore and I began fighting the system.

The company I was with simply used its employees to reach financial targets and they cared very little about people and their well-being. That didn't work for me, so I found myself defending my team from my boss.

I got into heated battles with my managers. I didn't stand back from their intimidation tactics. I spoke my mind. They weren't used to that and felt their superiority complex being challenged.

I was forced to resign, and again, my world was about to come crumbling down on me.

I had 2 week's notice and what I would stumble upon next would open a door to a whole new world of possibility...

5
A WHOLE NEW WORLD OF POSSIBILITY

"Rock bottom became the solid foundation on which I rebuilt my life"
—J. K. Rowling

Lobster

I was reading about when baby lobsters are born, they are born without shells. they are born vulnerable into the ocean, and over time, as their muscles strengthen, they then develop a hard outer shell.

And as they continue to grow on the inside, they eventually crack open the outer shell, again, leaving themselves vulnerable to their environment.

As they continue to grow, they again develop a hard outer shell, until they outgrow it, in which the crack it open again, leaving themselves vulnerable to their environment.

Over and over, through out their lives, they continue to crack open in order to grow…

I knew I had 2 weeks left with my team and I wasn't sure how to lead them in the time we had together. They had become family to me, and having to leave them was not going to be an easy task.

I felt hopeless. Lost without purpose. I had never felt so lonely in my life. I felt powerless. I knew I needed something, but I wasn't sure of what it was. It was a Saturday, and I woke up feeling a deep emptiness inside. I began to weep like a baby and the tears just came down like a waterfall.

I was angry, sad, unsure and heart-broken and I asked a few very important questions that would change the course of my life:

"Why am I here?"
"What is my life's purpose?"
"What's life about?"

(Remember these questions. They'll come into play a little later in the book.)

Fortunately, when we ask questions, we open the door to new possibilities to show up - **IF** we're open to receiving it. We live in a Universe that loves to support us and if we're willing to ask questions without going into conclusions, we access the power of the Universe.
(More to come on that.)

The next day, I found myself wandering in the Denver Public Library without a clue as to what was next for me.

I mindlessly picked up a few books here and there, but nothing grabbed me.

Then, I saw a section called "Personal Development" and it pulled me like a magnet.

I looked at some of the titles and something caught my eye:

Unlimited Power by Anthony Robbins

And as I opened the book and began reading, my whole being lit up! It was like I was reading something that I already knew, but was being reminded of.

In that book, the foundational teaching points are:

If you have a vision…

And you direct your physical, mental and emotional state toward that vision…

And you are willing to take massive action toward that vision…

You can create anything you want in life.

WHOA!!! That was a whole new concept for me. Something inside of me knew it was true, and I was ready to hear it.

We can only hear what we're ready to hear, and boy was I ready!

Unlimited Power, by Anthony Robbins, began to break me from the cultural hypnosis I was walking around in, and it opened up a door to a whole new world of possibility.

We are the absolute creators of our lives.

I read that 400 page book from front to back in just a week, and in my final week with that company, I didn't teach sales concepts or technology. I taught what I was learning from that book.

My team was looking at me like I went crazy, but I didn't care. I found the "secret" to life and I wanted them to know all about it. They were inspired. And this is where the Universe answered my question of *"why am I here?"*

On my last day of being with that company, 3 of my reps came up to me and said:

"You should be a motivational speaker..."
"You should be a motivational speaker..."
"You should be a motivational speaker..."

And by the 3rd time, I heard it! Something clicked! In my mind, I thought, *"OK!!"*

I even wrote each of them a mission memo, letting them know how much I cared and appreciated them.

It was very hard leaving them, but I knew I had grown out of that position and it was time for this goldfish to discover larger oceans to swim in.

I had a new vision, but it wasn't going to be easy. Could I *REALLY* go from being in the corporate world to being a motivational speaker? If so, how?

6
THE POTENCY OF VISION

"Everything happens twice. First in your imagination, then in reality."
-Albert Einstein

Lakshmi and Saraswati

The tale goes like this…

Lakshmi and Saraswati are brother and sister Hindu Goddesses.

Saraswati is the Goddess of knowledge, wisdom and creativity.

Lakshmi is the Goddess of abundance, wealth and prosperity.

When people *only* focus on pursuing Lakshmi without going through Saraswati, then Lakshmi is no where to be found.

When people focus on pursuing Saraswati, then Lakshmi shows up effortlessly.

Growing up, I had a vision to play professional football and when I shattered my leg, my vision vanished, which was one of the reasons I fell into depression.

I'm not a religious person, but there's a verse in the bible that says:

"Without a vision, people perish."

The mind and the Universe do not know the difference between something we vividly imagine and something we actually experience.

When my vision for my future was gone, I began to die inside. When I had my sales team I was managing, I had a new vision.

When that came to an end, I experienced the same thing - loss of vision.

It was the gift that my sales reps gave me of me being a motivational speaker that re-inspired me.

And now that this new vision was in place, I had the power of Universal forces in the palm of my hand.

Another book I read along the way that helped me become a motivational speaker and trainer today was:

Psycho Cybernetics by Maxwell Maltz

Maxwell Maltz was a cosmetic and plastic surgeon in the 1900's. He noticed that some of his patients would have radical transformations after undergoing cosmetic surgery, and some would not.

In many cases, once the outside appearance changes, the limiting internal self-image collapses. In other cases, the internal self-image is so strong, no matter how dramatic the external transformation, they can't see through the internal self-image.

Maltz was fascinated by this distinction and decided to study psychology and he became a pioneer in the arena of self-image.

In his ground-breaking book, he talks about the power of visualization as a way to enhance self-image and to visualize goals into reality.

After I read this book, I looked back on my football career. I had a routine before every game to imagine myself scoring touchdowns, breaking tackles and seeing me as a successful football player.

I was in awe that I had already implemented these tools without even knowing about them, and I was excited to see what was possible now that I could use them consciously.

So, with my new vision of becoming a motivational speaker, I went in to the theater of my mind and began to imagine myself in front of audiences.

I saw myself inspiring and uplifting people, and even though I had no idea "how" it was going to happen, it felt so amazing to be able to 'see' myself in that light.

Day after day I would go into my mind and visualize my future. To this day, I use visualization to help me create my desires.

Even though I knew I wanted to be a professional speaker, I simply wasn't ready, and when it was time to begin the interview process with other companies, I had a whole new set of tools to use!

I had some friends who were in the pharmaceutical industry and I thought I would try my hand at it.

So, as I was going through the interview process, I used my new visualization tools to help me get the job.

Again, I had no idea *how* visualization was going to help me get a job, but what did I have to lose?!

The fastest path to insanity, I've discovered, is trying to figure out *how* all the magic is going to happen.

So, before the first interview, I created the outcome I desired in my mind. I made it real in my body and felt the emotions as if it were happening.

I nailed the first and second interviews, but here is where the magic happened.

In my final interview, I was sitting in my car, in the parking lot, imagining the outcome as real. Seeing it and hearing him say *"Congratulations, you got the job"* and feeling the handshake.

I intensified it by using some of what I learned in Unlimited Power. I made the feelings stronger and stronger until I was emanating it.

The final interview was with my direct manager and the regional manager - the big guns! As the regional manager was asking me questions, I was cool and calm and answered each question with confidence and ease.

Of course, I was hired.

My direct manager and I had a dinner meeting shortly after that and here's what he said:

"George, when we were in the final interview and you were answering our questions, you were literally saying what I was thinking. It was the craziest thing..."

In my mind, I knew what happened. It was **The Power of Having a Vision**.

When we are clear with our vision, and we embody it with desire, the Universe provides the resources to make it real. Our job is simply to trust that what we need will show up on time and in perfect order. That's magic 101.

7
HOLDING THE VISION

*"What ever the mind of man can conceive and believe,
he can achieve."*
— Napoleon Hill

The FIRST

Apparently, Walt Disney never got to see Disney World open up. He passed away before the grand opening.

His nephew Roy Disney fielded all the questions from the press. At one point, there was a very arrogant reporter who asked Roy in a very nasty tone. He asked:

"Roy, how does it feel to know that your uncle Walt NEVER got to see Disney World open up?!"

Roy thought to himself for a moment and said:

"On the contrary sir. He was the FIRST to see it."

In my first few months of selling pharmaceutical drugs, I began to lose sight of my vision of being a motivational speaker. I got caught up in all the new tasks I had with my new position.

I didn't make the time to go into the theater of my mind to visualize. I was too damn busy…at least that was my excuse.

It was only when I was 4 months into my job that I realized I was feeling all those feelings of depression again because I wasn't *holding* the vision.

I immediately made time to visualize again and see myself in front of 100's and 1,000's of people.

Again, no clue how it would happen, I could just feel something activate inside of me every time I visualized.

I continued to study other personal development material to help me expand other areas of my life.

At the time, I really wanted to do well selling pharmaceutical drugs, so I studied a program called:

How to Win Friends and Influence People
by Dale Carnegie

Because I didn't believe in the products I was selling, I knew I had to win market share in my territory by out-working and becoming more liked than my competition.

I learned along the way that people do business with people that they know, like and trust.

So, I studied programs on charisma, charm, rapport and what I realized is that when we're simply being ourselves, people tend to like us.

Fortunately, I have natural communication ability and was able to win the Doctors Offices with my sincerity and hard work.

I adopted a territory that was operating at an average of 16% Market Share, so I had my work cut out for me.

In the first 6-months, I almost lost my job, but because my consistent hard work, and my newfound skills, I moved the market share in my favor by 8 points. That was big. My territory had not been over 20% in years.

I was relieved because I was feeling the heat from my bosses, and I was getting paid pretty well, which allowed me to take the next step toward being a motivational speaker. I used the money I was making to begin traveling around and attending live seminars and learning from the people I was reading about.

As I continued to build market share and expand my awareness and knowledge through personal and spiritual development, I knew I was coming to the end of my stay with selling pharmaceutical drugs.

I was 2 years into my position and was making more money than I ever had in my life...BUT, I felt the tug to resign and explore the world of personal transformation.

I left a comfortable 6-figure salary to pursue my new vision. Comfort is the killer of creation. Don't mistake comfort for flow. Flow is expansion in motion; comfort is coagulation and stagnation. Comfort will steal your brilliance and attempt to keep everything in your life the same. If you don't consciously and consistently break free from the comfort zone, in time, it will be the death of you and everything you are here to create.

8
ACTUALIZING THE VISION

"Take the first step in faith. You don't have to see the whole staircase, just take the first step."
— Martin Luther King, Jr.

Chipping Away

Michelangelo, who created the magnificent statue David, was asked how he created such a beautiful statue.

Michelangelo said,

"It was simple…I just chipped away at what wasn't David."

I had saved up a good chunk of change as the pharmaceutical rep and I decided that I was going to take the next 6-months and invest all of my savings into coaching certifications, speaking training, transformational events and whatever else it was going to take me to live my dream.

I held the vision and it was time to get into MASSIVE action. I read a ton of books, listened to tons of audio and been to a ton of events. I used those tools successfully in my job, and now it was time to test my skills in the pursuit of my vision of being a motivational speaker.

I heard a lot of things about NLP (Neuro-Linguistic Programming) from many people and so one of the first things I did when I resigned was take an NLP certification course.

I was in the mountains of Colorado for 2 straight weeks getting NLP certified. I learned how to help people create change quickly using this modality.

We worked on each other and helped each other create change in the areas we wanted to create change in. I was also certified in Hypnotherapy around the same time.

I learned all about how to communicate with the sub-conscious mind to create change at deeper levels. I was amassing a toolbox of skills that would come into play in the months ahead.

NLP taught me how powerful our communication is to ourselves. We all experience the world around us through our 5 senses - sight, smell, taste, touch and sound...

NLP stands for:
Neuro - Our Neurology
Linguistic - Communication (internal and external)
Programming - How we wire our brain to function in this reality

NLP helped me learn how our belief programs influence our thought patterns, which influence our feelings and emotions, which influence our behaviors and actions, which influence the results we create in our lives.

Beliefs — Thoughts — Feelings — Actions — Results

I learned all kinds of techniques and skills to help me break free from limiting thoughts, feelings and emotions. Here is a couple.

Anchors - An anchor is an emotional trigger that is set to a certain touch, sight, sound, smell or taste.

For example, think about a song that sets off a certain feeling…one that fires you up, makes you relax or makes you feel sexy…c'mon, you know you're sexy ;)

That's the power of anchors. They trigger certain feelings almost instantly.

While playing college football, I would always play Incubus' song '*Pardon Me*' before games and it would fire me up.

To this day, because I "anchored" that song to my mind and body to get fired up, I still get chills.

It's very much like Pavlov's dogs. Ivan Pavlov was a Russian scientist who was studying salivation in dogs.

Each time he would ring a bell, he would give the dogs some food. He did that over and over again until the he could ring a bell and the dogs would automatically salivate, because they were "anchored" to sound of the bell that food was on the way, which activated their salivary glands.

Can you think of the fragrance of cologne of your first love? Does it give you a certain feeling?

For most people, it does!

We are anchored in this reality like crazy, until we undo all the anchors and triggers that keep us hooked into the

Matrix. Anywhere you are triggered into a certain feeling or state of being, you're anchored. Whether it's a good feeling or bad feeling...Now, here's a simple way you can anchor yourself to a resourceful state of being:

1. Identify what state of being you desire
2. Think of a specific time when you were in that state of being i.e. funny, peaceful, enthusiastic, etc
3. Intensify it
4. Touch a certain part of your body or face that you rarely touch - like an earlobe
5. Repeat until the area you touch activates the state of being you desire

After a while, just touching your ear (or wherever you choose) will activate that feeling. Anytime I'm feeling stuck, I have a set of anchors that "pops" me into a resourceful state. But whatever you do, don't try it if you want to shift the way you feel quickly ;-)

Timeline - Timeline is some of the most powerful work I've learned in the NLP model. Essentially, in your mind, you can go back in time and add new resources to younger versions of you.

For example, think of a time that was lightly challenging for you growing up. Maybe a time when a younger you had a heart-break, or lost a dog, or broke your leg playing football.

When the current you, goes back and see's that younger version of you with the wisdom you've gained over time, you can consciously offer resources that the younger you, didn't have at the time.

Go back into time and see that younger version of you through the eyes of your love… If you take the time to do this exercise with versions of you in the past, you can help free those parts of you that may be energetically stuck.

Past   Now   Future

Note: *Timeline should be used by a trained professional when working with other people.*

One year before I started my business, I told people that I was already a coach and a speaker. I told people that I was an Emotional Awareness Coach.

I even made business cards, so I began living my future self, NOW. I began communicating to my brain and to the Universe that I was ALREADY a coach and a speaker.

That would help me condense time, because the mind doesn't know the difference between something you vividly imagine and something you actually experience.

Literally, the mind doesn't know what time is. When we embody what we desire, we collapse the concept of time and we begin to attract the people, circumstances, events, conversations, etc. that start to make that vision real.

I walked around, handing out business cards and telling people that I was an Life Coach and a Speaker. After saying and seeing it enough times, I began to believe it and as you already know, your beliefs create your reality.

I literally condensed time. Who knows how many years I shaved off, but it seemed to create a momentum that bent space and time.

Re-Frame - A re-frame is a powerful way to change the meaning of limiting experience.

It's very much like looking at the same experience from a different perspective or point of view.

Do you remember a movie you watched with a friend and one of you hated it, and one of you loved it? Same movie, different point of view.

When you look at an experience in your life that wasn't so pleasant, and begin to explore the meanings, beliefs, judgments and conclusions you've set up for it, you can free yourself from it.

For example, some cultures celebrate death as the beginning and other cultures look death as the end.

When I was forced to resign from my first job, I could have pointed the finger and blamed them for what happened. Even though it was painful, I chose to see that as a new platform that I could launch my life from.

Here are some great questions you can use to re-frame challenging experiences you've had, or are having:

What meaning am I giving to this that is disempowering me?

What else could this mean that would empower me more? Will this even bother me in 10 years?

Re-framing is simply the art of choosing an empowering meaning, versus a dis-empowering meaning to help free you from that limitation.

I teach and train many NLP classes, and if you are interested, visit my website (www.GeorgeIraCarroll.com) if you want to dive deeper into this phenomenal body of work.

There are also many books on NLP if you're interested in learning more, simply google: NLP Books, Seminars or Training and you'll get a lot of feedback.

When you're on the way to actualizing your vision, it takes action. And when you start taking massive action, that's when you're going to need these kinds of tools to help you break free from whatever limitations show up along the way. Now, it was time for me to take a leap of faith…

9
BUT WHAT IF I FAIL?

"Sometimes, your only available transportation is a leap of faith."
— Margaret Shepard

Jump

The man walked over to the cliff, and voice said, "jump."

The man said, "I can't, I'm afraid."

The voice said, "Jump...you can do it."

The man said, "What if I don't make it?"

The voice stood silent...

The man jumped...

And on the way down, he grew wings.

As I spent 6 months traveling, attending certification trainings and transformational seminars, it was time for me to make a choice. Do I start my business or do I get a job?

Well I simply wasn't ready to start my own business. I didn't know what I didn't know, and I was waiting for the perfect time. So, I jumped back into the corporate world and continued to chip away at my vision.

I was back in a similar field, so it was very easy for me to manage that job while I continued to pursue my vision.

After a few months of working with a medical marketing company, I realized there was never going to be a "perfect time" and at some point, there was going to be a time for me to take the leap into starting my business.

But I was afraid.

"What if I fail?"
"What if it doesn't work?"
"What if I'm not good enough?"

All the questions I had to face as I moved closer and closer toward my vision. What I've learned about human behavior is that, when what we are currently experiencing becomes more painful than the idea of moving forward and changing into the version of us we desire to become, we will move forward powerfully.

Being in the corporate environment was killing my spirit, and I knew I had to take the leap.

But I was afraid.

I had never built a business before. My past jobs were entrepreneurial in nature, but I had a salary to rely on.

I used my new tools to shrink my fear and negative *"what if's"* and one day, I made a deal with the Universe. I said: *"Alright Universe, here's the deal. You let me know without a shadow of a doubt when it's time to start my business, and I will."*

I spent 4-months in my new position and one day, as I was out for an intense run, it hit me loud and clear.

It was a flash of energy that I could not ignore or deny.

It was time. Was I ready?

10
THE BRIDGE TO DREAMS

"I think there is something more important than believing: Action! The world is full of dreamers. There aren't enough who will move ahead and begin to take concrete steps to actualize their vision."
— W. Clement Stone.

The Garden

A priest was walking through a neighborhood on a sunny day. As he walked by a beautiful garden, he stopped to admire it and had the urge to go tell the owner of the home what a great job the Lord has done with his garden.

So he walks un to the house, bangs on the door and a man answers the door and says,

> *"Hi priest, how can I help you?"*

The priest says, emphatically,

> *"I just want you to know that the LORD has done a good job with your garden!!"*

The man thinks for a moment…and says,

"You're right priest…the nursing sun, the life-giving water, the nurturing soil…you're right…but I do have to say one thing priest… YOU SHOULD HAVE SEEN THIS GARDEN WHEN THE LORD HAD IT ALL TO HIMSELF!!!"

The very next day, after my intense run, I went to the bank and registered my business account.

I purchased my domain name and went to work on creating a speaking and coaching website.

I created some generic business cards.

I went and rented some office space.

And with 2-months of savings and a vision, I took the leap!! I resigned from my job and I was off to the races!!

Wahooooo!!!!

Just 2 days before I started my business, I ran into an old friend and let her know what I was up to. She referred my first paying client!!

The Universe delivers fast!!

Guess what the name of my business was when I launched? Don't laugh too hard…

Inner Resonant Awareness

Yep, you read that right. What the hell does that mean?!! I had no idea!

It was an acronym for my middle name and I was studying a lot of internal change work, so that's where I started. I had to start where I was, and adjust the course along the way.

Remember, I didn't have any business experience, so I was just winging it. Fortunately, I learned something very powerful along the way that allowed me to shift and change quickly.

When I was taking my NLP training, I walked into a room of 45 people. I was timid and shy. I looked up the wall at a sign that said:

There is no Failure, Only Feedback

I began to cry. It was a shock to my belief in the idea of failure. It changed the way I looked at failure. Basically, this is a re-frame of the idea of failure. Every attempt simply provides feedback to use to move forward. Failure isn't possible unless we flat out quit for the rest of our lives.

So, after I started my business, the feedback I received from people on my business name wasn't magnetic enough. It was time for me to make a shift.

I then began calling myself a Hypnotherapist, and that scared the crap out of people even more. Great feedback for me to shift again.

Finally, I shifted into calling myself an NLP Coach and that seemed to stick. I was finally getting more paid clients. I was high on life!

My vision was at my fingertips and I reached out just a bit further, and I created my first speaking event. It was called:

The Structure of Interpersonal Communication

I know, sexy right...!? I had 14 people show up and my vision had become a reality!!

Well, on a small scale at least. But I was fired up! Years and years of imagining and envisioning and struggles and pains...it was now real!

And I wish I could tell you that I rode off into the sunset and I've been living happily ever after, but it was quite the opposite of that.

This is where it takes a turn for the worst...

11
BROKE, BED BUGS AND BANKRUPT

"In the end, you're only renting the stuff anyway."
— Anonymous

2 Wolves

An Indian Chief was sitting with a young indian boy and was sharing a story about 2 wolves.

The Indian Chief said:

"Inside all of us, there is a battle going on…a battle between 2 wolves…

…A wolf of love, compassion, peace, joy, happiness…

…and a wolf of hate, rage, anger, guilt, revenge…"

The young indian boy asked:

"Which wolf wins?"

The Indian Chief said:

"Which ever wolf you feed the most."

A few months into running my business, I got a few clients here, and a few clients there, but my 2-month savings had run out.

I held live seminars and even had up to 20 people show up, but I was running on fear.

Fear of being broke and having to go bankrupt.
Fear of failing.
Fear of being homeless.
Fear of having to go back to the corporate world.

I experienced the power that fear has when we choose to indulge in it.

I was feeding the wrong wolf....

I was coming off of having a $100,000 lifestyle and I watched as my life, and my business was sinking within the first year.

I had tunnel vision. I couldn't see the trees through the forest...

After 6 months, I moved into a 300 square-foot studio apartment in a "sketchy" part of downtown Denver. I minimized my life the best I could to try to catch myself from falling too hard.

I was frustrated. I had taken the leap of faith and acted when the inspiration hit, but I was obviously missing something.

What was it?

One day, I came home from hustling for clients and speaking engagements and I was frustrated almost to tears.

I dropped my bag on the chair and as I looked up, I noticed something jittering in my bed curtains.

I inched my way closer, with a look of disgust and curiosity draped on my face.

As I pulled open the bed curtain, I saw something that almost made me puke.

A patch of bed bugs that scattered in multiple directions.

I yelled, *"NOOOOOOOO!!!!!!!"* in despair…

There I was, living in a 300 square-foot studio apartment infested with bed bugs. The smell of failure reeked in my apartment, and I was crying my eyes out. Snot was running out of my nose and I could feel the gut-wrenching pain of self-judgment, disgust and blame.

I was broke as a joke, about to go bankrupt and homeless…Most of my belongings weren't salvageable, and I knew I was going to lose pretty much everything I owned.

I was devastated…and afraid. My spirit was defeated. I crumbled on my bed, wondering what the fu** had happened.

I was in massive judgement of myself, and in a split second, every tool I learned along the way was out of sight, and out of mind.

I was too busy being a victim…to God.

I was punching and screaming and crying…at God.

I yelled out:
*"I let go of everything I had so I could focus all of my time and energy on building my business and helping people and THIS is how you repay me? FU** YOU!"*

That's right - I was pissed.

Deep down, I knew it wasn't anyone's fault but my own, and I was the person I was most pissed off at.

But instead of taking responsibility, I pointed the finger and blamed everything and everyone I could point my finger at.

My parents
The government
My friends at the time
The apartment complex I lived in.

And then I started crying even harder. I simply could not see a way out.

I knew I had to get a job. I knew I was soon to be homeless. I knew that most of my belongings were rampaged by bed bugs.

I had a tunnel vision, and I just wept in my own self-victimization.

Then, in a fit of rage, I did the absolute best thing I could have done in that moment…

I ASKED A QUESTION!

It wasn't elegant, but it was the perfect question to ask in that moment…I asked:

"What the Fu** am I missing!!?"

What came to me in the moments ahead would forever change the direction and quality of my life…

12
A FLASH OF INSIGHT

"Gratitude unlocks the fullness of life. It turns what we have into enough, and more. It turns denial into acceptance, chaos to order, confusion to clarity. It can turn a meal into a feast, a house into a home, a stranger into a friend."
— Melody Beattie

3 Hairs

A woman had 3 hairs left on her head. As she woke up in the morning to do her hair, she said:

"What should I do with my hair today? I think I'll braid it."

So, she put her hair in a braid, and ha a great day.

The next morning she woke up with only TWO hairs left on her head. She said:

"What should I do with my hair today? I think I'll part it down the middle."

She parted her hair down the middle and had a great day.

The next morning she wakes up with only 1 hair left on her head. She said:

"What should I do with my hair today? I think I put it in a ponytail."

She put her hair in a ponytail, and had a great day.

The next morning, she wakes up with no hair left on her head. She said:

"Eh...at least I don't have to deal with my damn hair anymore!"

I remember watching a video of one of my favorite spiritual teachers, Wayne Dyer. He said:

"If you have food in the refrigerator, clothes on your back, a roof over your head and place to sleep. You're richer than 75% of the world. Just that...doesn't that call for some gratitude?

If you woke up this morning with more health than illness, you are more blessed than the MILLION who will not survive this week, because of illness.

If you have ANY money in the bank, you are among the top 8% of the world's wealthy...

When you consider our world from such a compressed perspective...it concludes that the need for gratitude becomes glaringly apparent."

Powerful. It rocked my world, and unfortunately, I didn't remember this awareness when I was in my pity party, BUT, I had enough awareness to muster out a question:

"What the fu** am I missing?"

That one question opened up an awareness that would change everything.

Within moments, a flash of insight hit, kind of like it hit me when it was time to start my business. The insight was...

Radical Appreciation

Immediately, a lightness washed over me. Something shifted so quickly and powerfully that my tears of anger, rage and blame, turned to tears of awareness and joy.

"OF COURSE!!", I thought.

I flashed back to all the material I had read on gratitude and appreciation. I remembered a powerful lesson I learned from Tony Robbins years and years back:

You don't know it unless you're applying it into your life. You can have an intellectual understanding of something, but if you're not actually implementing it into your life, you don't truly know it.

I had a great intellectual understanding of the power of gratitude and appreciation, but boy I was not applying it.

Gratitude…blah blah blah…

Appreciation…blah blah blah…

It was like the Charlie Brown cartoon, *"wha wha wha…wha wha wha"*

Even though I knew it in my head, I wasn't making it an everyday practice; therefore, I did not "know it".

That day changed everything. From that day moving forward, I committed to living my life from Radical Appreciation.

I began looking at life from a whole new perspective. I created a morning routine. I would go for walks as the sun was rising and with each step I said:

"Thank You...Thank You...Thank You...Thank You..."

I made lists of things I was grateful for.

I had $34 left in my bank account and I was grateful.

I had a car that barely worked and I was grateful.

I had a couple clients at the time and I was grateful.

I looked at everything in my life - the people, the stuff, the money, the business... EVERYTHING. And I found a way to be grateful.

I even found a way to be grateful for the bed bugs. I thought, *"I'm grateful that I can be a source of nutrition for these little guys."*

I didn't settle for the life I was living and I knew appreciation and gratitude were the way to a more free life - no matter what it looked like on the outside.

I had to claim bankruptcy because I was in way over my head and I didn't see a way I could make it back out. I had to get rid of all of my belongings because the bed bugs had moved in. I had to find a job, because I was not making ends meet.

I was on the verge of homelessness, because I couldn't afford the $495/month rent. 2 weeks after I realized I had bed bugs, my big brother Ray called me and said, *"Hey bro, what are you up to?"*

I said, *"Well, a lot of things. How about you?"*

He said, *"I just got a new place - come check it out!"*

I took a drive over and checked it out. He showed me a spare room and I asked him who would be living there. He said that it was a guest room and didn't have any plans for it.

The timing couldn't be better. We started chatting and catching up, and because he's an intuitive brother, he sensed something was off. He said, *"What's up bro?"* in that *big brother, are you okay* kind of tone.

I started tearing up, and told him what was happening. He told me I could live with him rent free until I got back on my feet. I started crying even more…because I was so grateful. I thought I was going to be homeless, but I was saved…this time around.

Now, did this show up as a result of me being grateful, or would this have showed up regardless?

I don't know, I was just grateful. I didn't need to know. If I was still in a crappy place of blame and self-judgement, would I have even taken that drive over? Would I have been in a place of receiving?

Who knows…I was grateful and that was enough for me.

On a beautiful, sunny summer day, as I was cleaning out the apartment I was living in, I sat down on a stump and looked over to see a baby squirrel that had fallen from the tree and was struggling to walk. It was shaking.

I went and grabbed a sock from my apartment, ran down and picked up the squirrel and brought him back up to the empty apartment.

I put him in a shoe box and crushed up some tiny pieces of banana with a side of sunflower seeds, topped off with a bottle cap of water.

He ate and drank.

I observed in gratitude, and I started crying.

That sweet little fragile squirrel taught me a valuable life lesson:

Life is Fragile. Live full out and be grateful.

As the day grew long, I decided to take him to a bushy area and placed him gently under a bush, in hopes that his mother would find him.

Maybe his mother found him. I don't know. He came into my life for a few brief hours to show me the beauty, gentleness and fragility that life could be, and it was time to be more grateful for life.

I remember the day - My brother and his sweet wife came to help me move the small amount of belongings I had.

I escaped being homeless by the hair on my chinny chin chin…for now.

Here are **5 Tools of Radical Appreciation** you can use to enhance the fullness of your life:

1. **Take walks, and with every step say out loud, or inside:** *"Thank You… Thank You… Thank You…"*

Then notice how you feel after word. Do it for a whole month and it just might change EVERYTHING!

2. Make lists of things you're grateful for

Look at your life - the people, the stuff, the money, the business, the job - EVERYTHING. Then start writing a list of reasons why you're grateful for them.

3. Make a Top 5 Gratitude People List

Who are the 5 people who have most impacted your life and call them and tell them how grateful you are for them. This one is an exponential-izer! Studies show that expressing gratitude to people is the fastest way to happiness.

4. Be Grateful for What You Desire

Remember, the Universe doesn't know what time is. When you are grateful for that which you desire, the Universe reads that you already have it. What is it that you desire, that you can start being grateful for now?

5. Write a letter to Money

Your relationship to money will largely determine how much flows to you. The more grateful you are for the money you have and for money in general, you begin to open portals for more to flow in. Imagine money is a good friend that you desire to have in your life. What would you say? How much gratitude can you show for it? Invite it to bring friends and come play with you more :-)

I wish I could tell you that gratitude alone was the answer, but it wasn't. In the months ahead, I would face a fork in the road that nearly derailed me from my vision.

13
IS GRATITUDE ENOUGH?

"When you come to a fork in the road.... Take it."
— Yogi Berra

Where are You Going?

Cat: *Where are you going?*

Alice: *Which way should I go?*

Cat: *That depends on where you are going.*

Alice: *I don't really know.*

Cat: *Then it doesn't matter which way you go."*

— Lewis Carroll, Alice in Wonderland

When I moved in with my brother, I had some breathing room to help get my business and life back on track.

I was grateful and that gratitude began shifting my life. I noticed more clients coming through my door and more people showing up to my workshops.

Most importantly, I had an inner peace that I hadn't had in a long time.

But gratitude wasn't enough to get me out of the rut I was in financially.

I had debt that I couldn't handle so I made the choice to claim bankruptcy. It wasn't an easy choice, but I made it.

I also had to get a job for $12 per hour making random cold calls to people asking them if they wanted to check their insurance rates.

Yes, I was THAT guy.

But I didn't care. I was just grateful that I could take a break and re-group myself so I could come back stronger.

I made lists of things I was grateful for. I went for gratitude walks. I was embodying Radical Appreciation.

I was at peace on the inside, but something was missing. Something was off and I couldn't figure out how to break free from just "getting by". Gratitude simply wasn't enough to help me thrive financially.

After watching my business go up and down like a roller coaster, I was tired. By the end of that first full year in business, I was ready to give up.

Yes, I was grateful, but I felt like I was holding myself back. Hitting a glass ceiling and I couldn't get past a certain financial level.

It was November of 2009, and I was at a crossroads. I wanted to give up. I was tired. I was frustrated. I didn't know if I had any gas left in the tank.

I began looking at my life and wondering what else was possible. I always wanted to live in Mexico, so I began looking at programs that would allow me to live in Mexico while I worked.

One day, it hit me! I can teach English as a second language to people in Mexico!

I started researching the steps I needed to take, and I literally began setting up my life so that I would move to Playa Del Carmen and teach English as a second language.

Underneath it all, I knew it was a way for me to avoid my true path of transformation in the world, but I wasn't listening to what was underneath. I just wanted a way out of my business because I felt like I was failing.

Just before I was about to make the investment to get certified and move down there, something inside of me said, *"Don't give up. Keep going..."*

When I heard that voice inside of me, I knew that I had to keep going. It was one of the most challenging times of my life. What was I going to do?

Have you ever almost given up on something, but somewhere deep down, you knew you had to keep going?

There's a certain pain in accepting your path and moving forward. An uncomfortableness that drove me to find out what needed to happen in order for me to have my dreams and vision.

I began looking deep within me and started asking some questions about where I was and where I desired to be.

I got dirt honest with myself and started looking at the basics of what I knew.

I asked, *"What creates results?"*

I re-connected with the basic concept:
Our *Values* and *Beliefs* create our *thought* patterns, which create our *emotional* patterns which create our *action* patterns which create our *results*.

Then, it hit me! What I became aware of next would give me the internal structure to go out and take my business to new levels.

When I had the awareness, it seemed so simple, but it wasn't easy to find until I took myself through this process that I'm going to teach you right now. I finally saw how I was limiting myself by holding on to old values that no longer served me.

I was 18 months into my business, and I was still doing the same things I was doing when I was first getting started.

Those things worked to get my business started, but to take it to a new level, I was going to have to do things differently. In order to do things differently, I was going to have to think differently.

In order to think differently, I was going to have to feel differently. In order to feel differently, I was going to have to shift my internal value system.

EUREKA!!

All I had to do was take a Value Inventory and identify what values I was currently operating from, and which ones were holding me back.

This was the AHA moment I was looking for, and as I began to re-wire my values, a new inspiration started to flow through me.

I started to see all the values I was still holding on to from childhood, exactly where they stopped me and how I could set myself free to have more success than I've ever had in my life.

I saw the light, and I immediately went to work that December, just before the New Year, and I started creating a whole new possibility for the next year.

What happened that very next year blew my mind and what you're going to learn in the next chapter will completely shift the trajectory of your life.

14
THE POWER OF VALUE ALIGNMENT

"The main benefit of knowing your values is that you will gain tremendous clarity and focus, but ultimately you must use that newfound clarity to make consistent decisions and take committed action. So the whole point of discovering your values is to improve the results you get in those areas that are truly most important to you."
— Steve Pavlina

Ham

A family was having Thanksgiving dinner one evening, and they were just about to serve the ham.

The mother was cutting both ends off the ham in a very large pan, and her 4-year old daughter was curious and asked, *"Mom, why are you cutting the ends off the ham?"*

She stopped to think, and said, *"sweetie, that's a good question. I don't know. All I know is your grandma always cut the ends off the ham."*

The little girl turns to her grandma and asks, *"Grandma, why did you cut the ends off the ham?"*

Grandma said, *"well, my mom used the cut the ends off the ham."*

The little girl turns to great grandma and says, *"Great grandma, why did you cut the ends off the ham?"*

Great grandma said, *"My pan was always too small!!"*

The Pain and Pleasure Model

Human beings are designed to avoid pain, and move toward pleasure. We will always find a way to repel what we deem wrong, bad, unjust or painful based on the experiences we've had with those specific areas of our lives.

For example, when the pain of having money is less than the pain of not having money, we will create more money in our experience.

We can say the same thing about relationships.

When being in a relationship is less painful than not being in a relationship, we'll find a way to attract a relationship into our lives.

As long as we associate more pain to the things we desire than we do pleasure, we will repel them. This is why having a vision that you associate pleasure to is far easier to achieve than a vision full of targets and goals that you associate pain to.

When the pleasure of what you desire becomes greater than pain associated to it, you'll tip the scales of having more of that thing in your life.

Keep this pain and pleasure model in mind as we explore your vision, targets/goals and our values.

Our values are handed down from the environment we grew up in. Like the mother cutting the ham, we are mostly unaware of the values that drive our every choice and behavior.

At the end of the day, what directs your life are the consistent choices you make. What influence your choices are your values and beliefs.

In many cases, we look to change our actions in order to get a greater result. We must understand that our values and beliefs drive our actions and are the core at what drives our behavior.

It's time to take an honest look at your current values, how some of them might be stopping you, and what values you need to take on in order to have what you desire.

When you do this, you will then have an internal GPS that will guide you to your targets and goals. Your targets and goals are what make up your vision.

A GPS works by having a destination. The GPS then calculates your relationship to your destination, based on where you are in the moment.

As you begin driving to your destination, your GPS will guide you every step of the way, until you eventually get there.

And if you take a wrong turn along the way, your GPS will "recalculate" and let you know where you can adjust your course.

When you have your vision in place, having an aligned value system will let you know when you need to recalculate. Below, write down your top 10 targets and goals for this year. Your targets and goals make up your vision.

Top 10 Targets/Goals for _____ (current year)

_____

_____

_____

_____

_____

_____

_____

_____

_____

_____

Here are some examples: A financial target, a relationship target, a weight loss or health target, a business growth target. Then, later in this chapter, you're going prioritize these targets, then you're going to choose the values that align with these targets.

Now that you have your top 10 targets/goals, the next step is to prioritize them. From most important to least important, list your prioritized targets/goals below:

_____

_____

_____

_____

_____

_____

_____

_____

_____

_____

By prioritizing your targets/goals, you will be clearer on how to organize your activities on a daily basis.

Now, it's time to identify what you currently value.

This part takes some inner exploration. Begin asking questions like,

What do I currently value based on my current behaviors?
What am I making important in my life based on what is showing up in my life?
Where am I consistently spending my time?

What is a value? Simply put, a value is what you deem important to feel or experience in life.

It's important to keep in mind that our values were "installed" in us from a very young age - our environment, parents and upbringing are the main source of our value systems, and here is the important key to remember:

Those value systems get us to a certain point in life, and when our life's vision changes, we must re-align our values so they move us toward our vision - not hold us back.

What your parents deemed as valuable is most likely the value system that you've taken on. But, the minute your vision changes, or gets bigger, some of your values may become out of harmony with your vision.

It's important to re-assess your values as often as your vision changes, or gets bigger. As you reach for bigger targets and goals, it's a good idea to align your values with them. Otherwise, your values will be in conflict with your vision.

Here are some examples of values:
- Comfort/Security
- Passion
- Health and Fitness
- Family
- Financial Freedom
- Growth
- Relationships
- Love

Value Conflicts

There are 2 instances when our values are in conflict:

In conflict with our vision - When your vision/desire is out of alignment or out-grows your value system.

In conflict with other values - When values conflict with each other.

In many cases, we will have Values in Conflict - That is when you have 2 values in conflict with each other.

For example, if you simultaneously value *growth* and *comfort*, you have a value conflict. Growth happens outside of your comfort zone and if your value for comfort is stronger than your value for growth, you will find a way to only grow as much as you're comfortable growing.

Limiting Values

Limiting Values are a HUGE key to understanding how powerful our values are.

A Limiting Value is a value you've taken on that limits you from having what you desire - your targets/goals and overall vision.

For example, let's say you have parents who have decided that rich people are a$$ holes (limiting belief). At some point in time, your parents made "lack or poverty" valuable to avoid becoming a$$ holes they judged rich people as.

Remember this:

We will unconsciously repel what we deem as wrong. And if we find a way to actualize it, we will find a way to get rid of it.

This is why people with poverty mindset who win the lottery become even more broke before they won the lottery 3-5 years later.

The Payoff

Some people value lack because the payoff is: avoiding being judged by others. Some people value lack because the payoff is: Fitting in with the masses. Some people value lack because the payoff is: Aligning with their parents world in order to gain approval, unconsciously.

The payoff is the underlying mechanism of what's being met that holds the limitation in place. We don't choose limitations because we like them so much, we choose them because we perceive them as vital to our survival.

Remember, most of this is not cognitive. Unconsciously, some people make the value of "Having money" a *bad* thing and so they find a way to rid themselves of it.

Anything you desire to have in your life, that you don't currently have, is the result of deep unconscious programming and cross-wiring of values and beliefs.

If you are creating "lack" in your life, it's because, on some level, you value "lack". There's a payoff underneath it somewhere. It has served some purpose in your life. The key is to understand what purpose it has served, so you can thank it, and choose again. Take a look at how you've set up the values in your life and write down below the current value system you have in place:

(CVS)Current Value System
List your current values below

_____

_____

_____

_____

_____

_____

_____

_____

_____

_____

Notice, which values are stopping you? Which values are supporting your vision? Which values are in conflict with each other? Which values are not aligned with your vision and targets? Make note of those Limiting Values below:

_____

_____

_____

_____

These Limiting Values are the values it is time to part with. With your vision and current values identified, it's time to re-write your values so that it matches your vision. Below, you will find space to write down the values that align with your vision and targets.

Aligned Value System (AVS) _____ (current year)

_____

_____

_____

_____

_____

_____

_____

_____

_____

Now, prioritize your values from greatest importance:

_____

_____

_____

_____

_____

_____

_____

_____

_____

Now you can make choices and take actions based on your new Vision and Values System. Can you see how doing this creates a powerful alignment within you?

When you have this in place, you will find yourself ON FIRE! This is the process I took myself through at the beginning of 2010, and that same year, I grew my business by 150%.

But I didn't do it by myself. One of the values I had on my list at that time was Faith in my knowing.

Sooner than later, I would have the chance to really practice that new value, and it wasn't what I expected…

15
THE POWER OF MENTORSHIP

"When the student is ready, the teacher appears"
— Buddhist Proverb

Walls

A young boy heard of a man who could walk through walls. So the young boy walked directly up to the home of the man, knocked on the door with authority and the man answered.

The man said, *"how can I help you?"*
The boy said, *"I hear you can walk through walls. Is this true?"*
The man said, *"Yes, that is true."*
The boy said, *"Will you teach me?"*
The man said, *"Yes, under one condition...I will teach you to walk through walls if you're willing to do everything that I ask."*
The boy said, *"Deal!"* with enthusiasm.

Months went by and the boy was asked to wash dishes and clean around the house.

After a few months, the boy approached the man said, *"Sir, I've been here for months now, and I still don't know how to walk through walls."*

The man said, *"be patient, your time will come."*

Another few months passed, and the boy approached the man said, *"Sir, I've been here for almost a year now, and I still don't know how to walk through walls."*

The man said, *"be patient, your time will come."*

One day, the boy was getting up to get some more wash rags and as he was walking, he walked straight through the wall, grabbed some rags, and walked straight back through the wall and continued cleaning...

As I started that next year, I felt ON FIRE with my new Vision and Value Alignment. Things were really picking up, and I could sense something BIG was going to happen soon.

In February, I was at a networking event, and the speaker was training on Social Media, so I assumed she was a Social Media Coach.

Later that day, we ran into each other and she introduced herself. A few seconds later, a friend of mine walked by and I introduced her as a "Social Media Coach" to my friend.

She gave me a dirty look and said, *"I'm not a Social Media Coach..."*

I said, *"Oh sorry, what do you do?"*

She said, *"I help people become celebrities in their industry."*

That grabbed my attention, and I said, *"Oh...we should talk."*

Later I learned that her brand was: **Born Celebrity**. And her name was Ingrid Elfver. A Swedish genius who had faced a near death experience that left her mentally imbalanced, living in a dark room for almost a year.

After she faced that, she said she became fearless and has now built a coaching and training business working with celebrities, and helping entrepreneurs become celebrities in their industry.

I was ready to become more of a celebrity. We scheduled a 1-hour consultation and after an hour of chatting with her on the phone, my intuition told me that working with her was going to be wicked expansive.

As we were wrapping up the conversation, she asked me: *"Do you have any questions for me?"*

I said, *"Nope, I'm ready - what's it going to cost me?"*

She said, *"Are you sitting down?"*

I said, *"Yes. Why?"*

She said, *"It's going to be $10,000 for a year.*

My body constricted and I went into scarcity thinking and said, *"I can't afford that!"*

She paused for a moment and said, *"George…that's your block. You have a money block. You're used to looking at your bank account and investing based on what you have, versus making a bigger choice and having FAITH that you have the ability and that the Universe has your back…"*

She was right. She and the Universe were testing my new value of *faith*. With $1,400 in my bank account, I put down the first payment of $1,000.

3 hours later, I had a potential client whom I had a consultation with a few months back call me to let me know he was ready to work with me.

I received 3 of these calls in the next few days and my first down payment had already paid for itself.

3 months later, my business had tripled and I was in awe. Here's what I began to realize.

I needed help. The perfect person showed up and I said yes to her because I was aware that my internal GPS was telling me to have Faith.

I finally opened myself up to receiving support and help from someone else. I had a belief in my head that said because I'm a coach, I don't need a coach.

Boy was I wrong. Here's something I learned from my friend Bob Burg.

"Money is an echo of value."

I was averaging $3,500 in my business at the time, and 3 months later, I had a $12,000 month.

Because I was willing to invest in myself, I was communicating something very powerful to my brain and to the Universe.

That I was worth investing in

When you invest in you, your value increases. When your value increases, so does the echo of income that starts to show up.

Please remember this. When you treat you with that kind of respect and appreciation, your value will appreciate and people will start seeing YOUR value, because you see your value.

Not only did my business triple, Ingrid helped me find a brand that was in alignment with my unique mix of energy.

Unleash Your Badass

I stepped outside the box of being an NLP Coach and became something greater. That brand helped catapult me into the next phase of my life and business.

It gave me permission to be more of me. It gave me permission to stand out and step up. That same year, I took my business from $40,000 to just over $100,000. I was on FIRE!

My seminar business doubled and I went from having 10-20 participants to having 30-70 participants.

My Vision of becoming an inspirational speaker was almost in full force, thanks to my Vision and Value Alignment.

The life I had envisioned years and years back, from being in the corporate world had almost come to fruition. I was now getting speaking engagements. I was living my dreams and my life and business was taking off.

I was finally able to move out of my brother's spare bedroom and eventually into a resort community in one of the most affluent parts of Denver - Cherry Creek.

I was living the life, and helping people…and getting paid for it. How does it get even better than that?

During that time, I was introduced to a body of work that would have me seeing the world in a whole new way…

16
LIVING IN THE QUESTION

"Questions create possibility. Conclusions create limitation."
— Gary Douglas

The Matrix Scene - Neo Meets Trinity

Trinity: *"I know why you're here Neo…I know what you've been doing…I know why you hardly sleep…why you live alone, and why night after night, you sit at your computer…*

…you're looking for him…I know because I was once looking for the same thing…and when he found me, he told me I wasn't really looking for him…I was looking for an answer…

…It's the question that drives us Neo…it's the question that brought you here…you know the question, just as I did…"

Neo: *"What is the Matrix…?"*

Trinity: *"The answer is out there Neo…it's looking for you, and it will find you…if you want it to…"*

As I began looking at how I could take my vision to a whole new level, I came across a body of work that changed how I looked at the world.

I was listening to an audio recording of a man named Dain Heer. He is the co-creator of a powerful body of work called Access Consciousness®.

This would be the beginning of a very transformative journey in my life.

As I was listening, I kept hearing him ask questions, and offering some killer wisdom like:

"When you ask questions, you create possibility. When you come to conclusions, you create limitation."

Something inside of me really connected with that idea. Dain also talked about the potency of caring and kindness. I never thought that kindness was potency. I was always taught that it was a weakness.

So, needless to say, the work triggered many of my concrete points of view that I was holding on to.

Initially, I was intrigued, and also resistant to the work.

I saw many people in the Denver community being taken by the work and many of them became certified facilitators

My curiosity pulled me in and I took a class here and a class there from people who were being certified by the work and I was simply unimpressed.

One day, I was driving down the street and my friend Katie texted me to tell me about an event that an experienced Access facilitator was putting on in Denver.

My mind wanted to say no, but my body said YES! Literally, I took a left turn to the hotel where the event was being held. It was like my body took over and started driving and I ended up at the evening event.

After the evening event was finished, I felt a tremendous lightness in my body and being, so I signed up for the rest of the 2 days. By the end of it, I started to see why so many people were gravitating to this work.

It's weird and kind of wacky, but if one is willing to open up and receive the work without barriers or judgement, there's no questioning its effectiveness in helping to eliminate limiting energetic patterns and limiting judgments.

Access has some foundational principles that can help people become more free from limitation.

For example, have you asked yourself what would you create if you had no past reference points?

Realllllly think about that one...

Feel that...? That's called space and possibility.
Maybe you don't feel it...but maybe you can sense it?

The challenge is, we've been taught at a very young age that
it's important to have the right answers.

Most of our entire educational system is based on how
many "right answers" we have.

One of the most brilliant people on the planet said:
"Question everything..."

That was Albert Einstein. Albert Einstein also said,
"Imagination is more important than knowledge."

By being curious, we activate our imaginative capacities. By
asking questions and *living in the space of the question*, we
invite the Universe to help us create magic.

The challenge is, we're taught to come to conclusions. In
fact, the traditional schooling system is designed to reward
kids with the right answers.

From Kindergarten through High School, the system
judges based on right and wrong. The more right answers
you have the better grades you get. The better grades you
get the better chance you have at getting a great job.

And when we leave the schooling system, we're left with a pattern of looking to get life right, versus having a creative adventure!

What would it take to change the entire school system so that it fosters the brilliance within our children?

Having conclusions gives us a sense that we're doing something right, so that we can control the outcomes of our reality.

Let me ask - would you rather have all the right answers, or live in a world of infinite possibilities?

Always question what's not working in your life. Not from a place of the wrongness of you, but from a place of curiosity.

The thing is, we're asking ourselves questions every day, but most of our questions are dis-empowering.

Many people have a habit of asking questions like, *"What's wrong with me?"* or *"Why am I so stupid?"*

These are not the questions that will help free you. Your brain is very much trained to be like Google. When you type in a search term in Google, you get gazillions of answers.

What if you just asked questions around all the areas that aren't working in your life? Questions like, *"What else is possible that I have not even considered?"* and *"How does it get any better than this?®"*

These are questions that I've learned through Access, and they have helped me create a whole different world of possibility.

To live in possibility, what we have to do is re-train our brain to not come to conclusions and that can take some time, but what *would* it take to live in the question more often? What could life be like if you allowed yourself to let go of needing to have an answer?

Could you be more free?

What would you have to let go of to be more free?

Do you try to control your life to turn out a certain way?

What if the Universe knows more about what we really want than we do?

Would you allow the Universe to deliver it?

Here's what most of us are taught about living a successful life:

Go to school.
Graduate from High School.
Get a College Degree.
Get a good paying job.
Get married. Buy a house.
Have kids.
Get a raise.
Raise a family.
Climb the corporate ladder.
Save for the future.
Retire.
Die.

Hmm…what else is possible here? Whose life are you living? Is it yours? Is it *really* yours?

Just something to consider. If you're not doing the work you love, it's probably not *your* life. If you were choosing for you…TRULY choosing for you, what would you be choosing? How would you be living?

For some people, exploring that possibility is like that *other* scene in the Matrix, when Morpheus shows Neo what the Matrix really is.

Neo comes out of the Matrix and into the "real world" puking because it was such a shock to what he thought the world really was.

When we start to ask ourselves questions like, *"Whose life am I really living?"* - We start to sense something that most people don't want to become aware of.

For most people, to truly live the life they came here to live, it would mean a complete overhaul and de-construction of their current life. And most people don't want to go through that uncomfortableness.

They would much rather tolerate the life they've created because they can control it. It's familiar. But, what's the value of controlling what's not working?

And don't get me wrong, your life may be amazing and you may totally be in love with what you're doing in life. Awesome! Keep doing it!

If your life is *not* working the way you desire it to, maybe it's time to ask some new questions? Only you know. And please know, there's nothing wrong with your life right now.

Your life is exactly where it is, and if you desire something different, you must be willing to be and do something different. You must also be willing to ask some questions to open up new possibility in your Universe.

Are you willing? You don't have to. In fact, you don't have to do anything different. It's all just a choice.

And when I decided to take my life to a new level, I had a new set of tools in the form of questions to help me do just that. Access also offers tools to clear those old limiting points of view. It's a great body of work.

I began asking questions like:
"What would it take to travel the country and speak?"
"How can I take my message to a national scale?
"What have I not considered here?"
"Where else can I look for more national exposure?"
"Who might discover me to help me go national?"
"What are the infinite possibilities to be a national speaker and trainer?"

All of these questions were inspired from the work I had done with Access, and what they helped me create next was pretty magical.

17
LOCAL TO NATIONAL

"You will either step forward into growth, or backward into safety."
— Abraham Maslow

The Swan

A Swan from the great oceans of the north had retreated south for the winter. When winter was over, he lifted himself into the air to fly back to the north.

A couple of days into his journey north, he decides to take a rest next to a pond. As the Swan landed, he was met by a Frog.

Arrogantly, the Frog asked: *"Who are you and where are you from?"*
The Swan said: *"I'm a swan and I'm from the great oceans of the north."*
The Frog said, *"Great oceans?! How big are these oceans?"* As he took one hop backwards, he asked, *"Are they THIS big?"*
The Swan said, *"No dear friend, they're much bigger than that."*
The Frog took 2 hops back and asked, *"Are they THIS big?"*
The Swan said, *"No dear friend, still much bigger than that."*
The Frog hopped all the way around his pond and asked, *"Are they THIS big?"*
The Swan said, *"No friend, still much bigger than that."*
The Frog said, *"You're a LIAR and a FOOL!"* Because the Frog knew that nothing was bigger than HIS pond...

The Swan shrugged his shoulders and lifted himself into the air, and headed back the great oceans of the north...

One thing I've learned along the way is that there are 2 primary states of being:

Contraction and Expansion

We are living organisms. If we're not growing, we're dying. Every step we take into the unknown expands us beyond where we've been.

The challenge is that most people have become comfortable and stagnant. If we're not constantly stepping into the unknown, we are slowly shriveling into our own black hole of comfort.

When people get too comfortable, it becomes harder and harder to step out. That is why consciously choosing to go outside of our comfort zones is the fastest way to growth.

Jack Canfield once said, *"Everything you want is outside of your comfort zone."*

Where in your life are you unwilling to step into the unknown? What step is it time to take, that would give you the adventure of life and living?

I was getting comfortable with doing local training and speaking and I was ready to take my vision to a new level. wanted to travel around the country and speak and teach people concepts that had helped free me to live my dream.

I connected with monster.com and began traveling and speaking to High Schools for one of their college preparation programs.

During this time, I also contracted with a speaking bureau that would help take my work nationally.

Within just a few years of starting my business, I was a National Speaker and Trainer. Who would have guessed!!?

I was doing what I love and making great money! Cities like Chicago, San Francisco, San Diego, Seattle, Denver, Dallas, Philadelphia - I was hitting all the big cities and I was creating relationships all over the US.

I was ON FIRE!

One day, as I was driving, I realized that my vision had become real. I was looking back, seeing that depressed, hopeless version of me that I once was and I had totally transformed that version of me into BEING the vision I created out of the depths of desperation for a better life.

After my events, I had people coming up to me and asking for my autograph and thanking me for the training.

I couldn't believe it! I was becoming somewhat of a celebrity!

I started delivering trainings for some of the top
companies in the US:
- American Family Insurance
- Capital One
- Monster.com
- Keller Williams Realty
- Colorado Association of Realtors

I began making BIG strides and I was training for
audiences up to 200 people.

Of course, like our friend, the Frog, we never want to be
satisfied with where we are. Grateful, yes. Satisfied, never!

Successful and fulfilled people have an insatiable appetite
for growth and expansion. They have a hunger for more,
while being radically grateful for where they are.

As a result of all of the training I was delivering, my 1-on-1
coaching practice exploded.

I was using my speaking engagements and my seminars as a
way to funnel people into my coaching programs.

I was literally so busy that I couldn't take on any more 1-
on-1 clients. So, I took the next step in my business -
Leveraged Group Coaching programs. I developed a
Mastermind Program designed to leverage my coaching
skills.

I was making more money than I ever had in my life, and I was helping tons of people be inspired and create a business that was producing more income.

I worked with a client who came to me and was barely making ends meet. She was a single mother and having to pull from her savings to pay her mortgage. She was a powerful change agent, but unable to create a business that generated the income she desired around her gifts.

After about 4 months of working together, we shifted her target audience to women. We shifted her expertise to coaching women in parenting and relationships.

We created coaching packages that made it easy for her potential clients to say yes. Within 6-months, she had an $8,000 per month income and helping more people create positive change in their lives.

I get this all the time. Women (and some men) who have a powerful gift to help people and change lives and make a bigger difference in the world, but so many limiting beliefs around business, money, selling, marketing and self-worth.

When I work with people, I first work on their fixed beliefs, judgments, conclusions and points of view that keep them stuck. We blow those away, then we begin creating an amazing business around who THEY are, and their strengths and gifts.

By the end of 2012, I had my best year ever in all areas of my life and business, and I was living into the vision I created when I was broken, battered and beat up.

I believe our greatest gifts are born in the depths of our despair. If we're willing to dig deep in those moments of uncertainty and struggle, we can get a glimpse of the magic that gets created when we are in our darkest hour. With every limitation we experience, we create the equal and opposite energetic possibility. This isn't hope or philosophy, this is energy and physics.

Without those times of depression, hopelessness and uncertainty, I wouldn't have tapped into the birthing of a greater vision for my life.

But, because change is inevitable and in order to create an even BIGGER life, we sometimes must de-construct the old one.

In the following year, my life would change in ways that I couldn't have predicted...

18
THE BEGINNING OF EGO-DECONSTRUCTION

"When it's all said and done, our ego parts are simply wounded children stuck inside of us, needing to be nurtured, loved and reminded that everything is ok and that there is another way to operate in the world."
— George Carroll

Screw

A manager was working in a factory that built and shipped goods to customers. One day, all the conveyor belts that took the packages to the correct trucks for delivery all of the sudden stopped working. The manager freaked out, called his mechanical guys to come over and fix it. 10 minutes later, the mechanical guys showed up and slowly begins looking around. The manager knows that thousands of dollars are being lost every second as a result of the conveyor belts not working.

After about 10 minutes of slowly making his way around the factory, the mechanical guys see's something odd in a small cabinet. He leans in to take a closer look, pulls out a screw driver and turns that one screw a quarter of an inch…all of the sudden, everything turns back on and the conveyor belts are working again.

The manager is excited!! He says, *"Thank you, thank you, thank you! How much do I owe you?"*

The mechanical guy says, *"$10,000"* without a flinch.

The manager says, *"WHAT!? You were here for 10 minutes. I want to see an itemized bill."*

The mechanical guy writes the itemized bill out on the sticky note, and gives it to the manager. The manager takes a look at it, smiles and writes him a check for $10,000.

The sticky note said: Turning screw: $1.00
Knowing which screw to turn: $9,999

Sometimes, it's the smallest the things that make the biggest difference. One choice can change the whole trajectory of one's life.

In 2006, I visited San Diego, California for the first time. I was in love.

The weather, the ocean, the nightlife, the people, the beauty. I just knew at some point I was going to live there. I continued to visit every 4 or 5 months to get in the energy of it.

While I was there, I would go visit luxurious condos for sale, getting myself to really feel the energy of what it would be like to live there.

On my early vision boards, I had images of San Diego pasted all over it. I knew I was going to live there someday.

Every time I had to leave, a small part of me was sad, because I knew I wasn't going to be back for months.

I continued to visit. I didn't know "how" it was going to happen, but I just kept the vision. Very much like what I did with becoming a motivational speaker and trainer.

Over time, I had built my business to a place where I could live almost anywhere, but it would mean that I would have to take my coaching programs online.

One day, in 2012, while I was visiting San Diego, I had the energetic hit that it was time for me to move.

So, I began doing all the things necessary to make it happen. I let the resort complex I lived in know that I was moving. I began looking for apartments in San Diego online and within a couple months, everything was set.

I even stopped traveling and training, which was the most fun for me in my business.

My move in date was December 17, 2012. When you move on inspiration, things happen fast!

So there I was, living in a new city. A city I longed to live in for years. I moved most of my business online, but there were a couple of Group Coaching Programs that I still had in Denver that I would fly in for every month.

I was so pumped to be in San Diego and I lived right in the heart of downtown.

But there was something lurking underneath the surface, and I wasn't aware of it.

I was making the transition of moving my business online. If you've ever experienced the work that I do, you know how much I love being with people, in person.

I remember seeing all of these internet marketers and internet entrepreneurs making tons of money online, and so I began trying to create my business like theirs.

This was the beginning of the collapse for me. I was veering away from my values to try to be like internet entrepreneurs, not realizing I was leaving my values behind. The beauty of it all was that I was learning some very important internet marketing strategies that I didn't have, which helped me tremendously.

I knew it was time for me to begin looking for another mentor, to help take my business to new heights. By February of 2013, I was was rockin' and rollin' and most of my business was online.

But something was *off*. What was it?

I didn't care. All I wanted to do was make money online. That was my focus at the time. And sure, I also wanted to help people, but I was too engulfed in creating a lifestyle instead of making a difference.

I ended up taking a trip to Kuala Lumpur for an event called Money and You. It was one of the most powerful 4-day events I've ever attended on business and life transformation.

I was more committed to investing in myself in 2013 than ever. I knew that if I kept investing in myself, the returns would eventually show up.

I didn't realize at the time that I was investing in myself from a place of wanting more money, not adding value to my business. Small distinction. Big mistake.

Kind of like our mechanical guy with the screw-driver. A small distinction, but in the long run, it would make a huge difference. Stay tuned…

I bought an online program called 6-Figure Tele-Seminar Secrets and I studied it like crazy. Lisa Sasevich is the creator of this program.

I started to follow her program, step-by-step and I could see how I could literally have a 6-Figure launch with her program.

I saw $$$$$$ signs!

In that program, she offered a free ticket to her live event in May of 2013, so I planned a trip to Vegas to go see her.

When I arrived at her event, I felt something special. I had attended other events that were being held by Coaches and Entrepreneurs I was looking to hire as my mentor, but no one had given me the energetic "hit" I was looking for.

Until I entered Lisa's event room, I had the emotional and energetic hit! I began to tear up before the event even started, and I knew I was going to be working with her on some level.

As the event went on, I continued to receive more and more value from her work. She finally got to the point where she was talking about her high level programs.

To join her Mastermind, I would have to invest $24,000. Ouch. Again, I was faced with another big choice. Do I keep doing what I'm doing, or do I invest in someone who can help me grow? I followed my gut and I paid the down payment of $3,000. Again, I was excited, but little did I know, something was brewing underneath the surface. I didn't even know it was there. It was a blind spot.

After the event, I was ready to launch my online program called, The Client Magnetism System. It's a 90-day online training course designed to help Coaches and Change Agents build their coaching business from the ground up.

I put a lot of heart and soul into this program. I invested in technology that would help propel me to a whole new level.

I hired a virtual assistant and a web-designer to help me launch. I did everything Lisa's program listed out and by the end of the launch, I had grossed $27,000. SUCCESS!!

But there was one problem…I was totally burned out. I was tired from the 18-hour days I was putting in, and I needed a break, but I couldn't take one.

Over the course of the 90-days, I would deliver the program and it was a massive success. People loved it, and I actually loved delivering it.

During the 4th of July weekend, I was powerfully drawn to another Access Consciousness event that Gary Douglas was facilitating.

Gary is the Founder of Access and a very powerful healer and transformational artist. This is where the course of the rest of my life would change, and it was not comfortable.

During that 4-day event, I would open myself up to healing an ego part of me I didn't know was there. This was my blind spot.

Here's what we have to remember - when we create our lives from ego, those parts of our lives never last because those parts of us aren't real.

When the ego creates, it's not sustainable, because eventually, as those ego parts of us are healed and integrated, everything associated to it on the outside world begins to crumble.

Ready for this? This is what was lurking underneath the surface I've referred to as my blind spot. My blind spot was that I was building my business from an ego part of me that was based in need, proving and fear.

These "parts" of us are unconscious parts that have been separated from our wholeness at some point.

They can be powerful creative forces, but when they are healed and integrated back into our wholeness, they no longer have creative powers, unless we keep choosing them.

During that 4-day event, Gary facilitated me through some powerful work, and I remember him saying:

"George, in order for the greatness of you to show up, everything that's not the greatness of you has to die. Are you willing to allow what's not the greatness of you to die?"

I said, *"Yes."*

He also said, *"If you truly want to have it all, you have to be willing to lose it all."*
(Remember this for later…)

Then, he worked his magic on me and everyone else in the room and the transformation that had taken place was one that was irreversible. When I got home from it, I spent the next 4 days in bed, feeling raw and exposed.

Everything *that* old part of me had created was about to come crumbling down. This would be one of the most uncomfortable chapters in my life. That part of me was dying and there was nothing I could do to stop it, but it would do it's best to stay alive.

Our ego parts are very persistent. They survive on *our* belief in *their* stories, lies and the illusions they make up about the world, other people and what we have to do to survive.

The ego is a master manipulator and many people go their whole lives with their ego creating their lives, instead of consciously creating from the infiniteness that we all are.

This part of me was operating from a lie of needing to prove it was worthy through the accumulation of money. Underneath that lie was the wound. The wound of feeling insecure about me and indulging in the lie that money could actually fill that hole inside of me.

Most of my life, I felt insecure about myself, and this ego part of me attempted to feel significant by trying to make more and more money. I began to see how some people are rich financially, but miserable on the inside, because they haven't dealt with the ego parts of them that are still operating on using money as a way to feel significant.

When it's all said and done, our ego parts are simply wounded children stuck inside of us, needing to be nurtured, loved and reminded that everything is ok and that there is another way to operate in the world.

Gary helped me see that, and helped me heal one of the most wounded parts of me that I was unwilling to face, until that event.

But remember, we can heal, and we still have a choice to operate from awareness, or ego.

What would I choose? The aftermath of that event would begin to catalyze me into an adventure I wasn't sure I was willing to have…

19
SURRENDERING CONTROL

"Seek the wisdom that will untie your knot.
Seek the path that demands your whole being."
— Rumi

Burn the Ships

A commanders led his men to battle on an island they were going to take over.

As the 3 ships land on the island, all the men empty the ships and begin to prepare for battle.

The commander stays behind as the men settle into their fortresses, and he lights the ships on fire.

As the flames become so big, the men notice what the commander had done. They begin shouting at him in anger, wondering what he was doing.

The commander calmed the men down and in a commanding voice, he said, *"Either we win, or we die."*

Access Consciousness was instrumental in helping me collapse my ego structures. In October of 2013, I attended an event called: Being You, Changing the World that Dr. Dain Heer facilitates all around the world.

If you've ever met Dain, you know what a gift to humanity this man is. The event took me into even deeper levels of collapsing ego parts of me that were in the way of me having my greatness.

Dain brought me on stage and took me through his process called Energetic Synthesis of Being - a transformational energetic process that profoundly demolishes limitations, if the person is willing.

And I was willing. This was one of the most transformational events I've ever attended. After that event, I felt a freedom that I've never felt before. It was also another level in healing my ego part that looked for significance through money attainment.

My lease in San Diego was up on November 5, 2013. I had about 45 days to figure out what my next move was. After the Being You event, I knew what I was being guided to do but I didn't want to face it.

One day I was sitting at the beach, pondering what was next for me and it hit me - I remembered Gary Douglas saying, *"In order to have it all, you have to be willing to lose it all."*

And in that moment, I knew I was going to be embarking on an adventure that would force me to face my deepest fear…

Our deepest wound lives in the illusion that we are unlovable, or unworthy of love. There's no deeper lie than the idea that our essence isn't worthy of itself.

The layers that cover that up are just scabs that cover up the initial wound. To heal, we must follow the thread of pain down to the root illusion, become aware of it and unplug it.

Deep within us all lives the limitless possibility of total freedom. Freedom from fear. Freedom from illusions. Having total awareness. Freedom to express our uniqueness without filters. Being fully actualized in a human body.

And I simply will not stop until I am the embodiment of this. I am willing to die to have this, and BE it in this lifetime. Not just for me, but for humanity. To be an example that we can be free, no matter what our external world looks like. Nothing will stop me.

We are all Gods in human form. There's no reason to not remember this truth. We didn't come here to be human. We came here to live in human bodies and to create like Gods create. Infinitely, powerfully and magically.

No more hiding. No more watering ourselves down to appease the masses. It's time to live out loud, and be our badass selves, fully expressed in all of our glory.

It's time to end the madness of limitations. NOW. Not later. NOW. The world literally depends on us stepping outside of limitations and creating a new world based on what's possible for the whole, not just for the individual. I was looking at my deepest fear straight in the face. What was my deepest fear, you might ask? Here it is…

The fear of poverty…

Wait, it goes deeper. Underneath the fear of poverty was… The fear of what people would think about me if I lived in poverty…

Wait, it goes deeper. Underneath the fear of what other people would think about me if I lived in poverty… The lie that being in poverty would make me unlovable…

I had an underlying belief that the stuff I owned and the amount of money I had determined my value and worth, and the Universe was strongly inviting me to surrender all of it…

Remember, our deepest wound is that we are not lovable, and this was the thread I followed to reach that awareness. The next step for me was to fully embody living homeless as a way to face my fear of living in poverty, and break free from that bullshit illusion. It's one thing to know what your greatest fear is. It's another to live it.

One of many things I learned from Anthony Robbins is, to break free from a fear, we must give ourselves experiences that contradict the fear.

By facing my fear of living in poverty and being homeless forced me to face everything in the way of me having total inner freedom.

It was time. I was terrified.

20
THE JOURNEY INTO HOMELESSNESS

"Expose yourself to your deepest fear, after that, you are free."
— Van Morrison

On November 5th of 2013, I sold most of my belongings, and was left with 2 suitcases and a car. Where would I go? How would I keep my dream alive?

This was just the beginning…

In the months that would follow, I would come face to face with my deepest and darkest fears, and it would be the most daunting challenge of my life.

There are times in life when the Universe has plans for you that you cannot and should not avoid; where a portal into a greater version of you resides. This was one of those times for me…

One of my favorite sayings goes like this… *"When nothing is certain, everything is possible."*

21
A Hero's Journey

To Be Continued...

"The cave you fear to enter holds the treasure you seek."
– Joseph Campbell

BOOK GEORGE TO SPEAK AT YOUR NEXT EVENT, CONVENTION, RETREAT OR CONFERENCE

Would you like to book George for your next event? Visit www.GeorgeIraCarroll.com/Book-George to explore the possibilities of bringing George's expertise, experience and passion to you!

ABOUT THE AUTHOR

George Carroll, also knows as a Transformational Artist, has trained for organizations such as Capital One, American Family Insurance, Colorado Association of Realtors, Monster.com and Lawyers with Purpose. George spent many of his years chasing his dreams of becoming a professional football player, until he shattered his leg and ankle during his senior season, leaving him depressed and hopeless.

George moved to Denver, CO and excelled in corporate sales and management, but he was left unfulfilled and empty inside. He resigned from a comfortable 6-figure salary knowing something greater was possible. He turned to the human potential movement seeking healing, growth and transformation. As a result of his own transformative experiences, his passion to help others on their journey of transformation was ignited. He eventually started his own speaking, training and coaching business.

Now, George is a sought after speaker, trainer and facilitator and delivers live events, corporate training and online programs all over the world. His wisdom and laser coaching style, in addition to his playful and fun-loving personality, makes him an ideal facilitator and speaker for your next event, convention, conference or retreat.

RECOMMENDED BOOKS

Personal Transformation:
Unlimited Power - Anthony Robbins
Awaken the Giant Within - Anthony Robbins
Psycho Cybernetics - Maxwell Maltz
The Alchemist - Paulo Coelho
Neuro-Linguistic Programming for Dummies
NLP: The New Technology of Achievement - Charles Faulkner
Heart of the Mind - Connirae Andreass
Transform Your Self - Steve Andreas
Frogs into Princes - Richard Bandler
My Voice Will Go With You - Milton Erikson
Being You, Changing the World - Dr. Dain Heer

Business:
Purple Cow - Seth Godin
Joy of Business - Simone Milasas
4-Hour Work Week - Tim Ferris
Good to Great - Jim Collins
Invent it, Sell it, Bank it! - Lori Greiner

Money and Finances:
Think and Grow Rich - Napoleon Hill
Money Isn't the Problem, You Are - Gary Douglas & Dain Heer
Secrets of the Millionaire Mind - T. Harv Eker
How Rich People Think - Steve Siebold
Rich Dad, Poor Dad - Robert Kiyosaki

Made in the USA
San Bernardino, CA
09 November 2014